Humpback Whale
The Singer

by Natalie Lunis

Consultant:
Mary Ann Daher
Security & Technology Control Officer
Woods Hole Oceanographic Institution
Woods Hole, MA

BEARPORT
PUBLISHING

NEW YORK, NEW YORK

Credits

Cover and Title Page, © Francois Gohier/Photo Researchers, Inc. and idreamphoto/ Shutterstock; TOC, © Jordan Tan/ Shutterstock; 4–5, © Minden Pictures/SuperStock; 6, © Walker Historical Picture Archive/Alamy; 7, © The Granger Collection, New York; 8, © Chris Johnson/Ocean Alliance; 9, © Minden Pictures/SuperStock; 10, © age fotostock/SuperStock; 11T, © Karina Wallton/Shutterstock; 11B, © David B. Fleetham/SeaPics; 13, © Masa Ushioda/Image Quest Marine; 14L, © David Tipling/Nature Picture Library; 14R, © Minden Pictures/SuperStock; 15, © Minden Pictures/SuperStock; 16, © Flip Nicklin/Minden Pictures, Photo obtained under NMFS permit; 17, © John Hyde/AlaskaStock; 18, © Mark Carwardine/npl/ Minden Pictures; 19, © Michael S. Nolan/SeaPics; 20, © Masa Ushioda/SeaPics; 21, © James D. Watt/Image Quest Marine; 22T, © Slavoljub Pantelic/Shutterstock; 22B, © ECOSTOCK/Shutterstock; 23TL, © Mark Carwardine/npl/Minden Pictures; 23TC, © Minden Pictures/SuperStock; 23TR, © John Hyde/AlaskaStock; 23BL, © Michael S. Nolan/age fotostock; 23BR, © Danny Frank/Image Quest Marine.

Publisher: Kenn Goin
Editorial Director: Adam Siegel
Creative Director: Spencer Brinker
Cover Design: Dawn Beard Creative and Kim Jones
Photo Researcher: Picture Perfect Professionals, LLC

Library of Congress Cataloging-in-Publication Data

Lunis, Natalie.
  Humpback whale : the singer / by Natalie Lunis.
    p. cm. — (Animal loudmouths)
  Includes bibliographical references and index.
  ISBN-13: 978-1-61772-280-6 (library binding)
  ISBN-10: 1-61772-280-4 (library binding)
  1. Humpback whale—Juvenile literature. 2. Animal
sounds—Juvenile literature. I. Title.
  QL737.C424L86 2012
  599.5'25—dc23
                           2011019011

For more information, write to Bearport Publishing Company, Inc., 45 West 21st Street, Suite 3B, New York, New York 10010. Printed in the United States of America in North Mankato, Minnesota.

073011
042711CGE

10 9 8 7 6 5 4 3 2 1

Contents

Underwater Song

Deep down in the ocean, a loud series of noises begins.

The moans, grunts, squeals, and roars go on for 20 minutes or so.

Then they repeat over and over in the same way for hours.

Together, the loud, strange noises make up the song of the humpback whale.

It is the longest and most complicated song of any animal on Earth.

When a humpback whale sings, it usually hangs head down and tail up in the water, holding its flippers out to help it stay in place. Sometimes, however, humpbacks sing while swimming underwater.

A Mystery at Sea

Sounds that are made underwater usually cannot be heard in the air above.

In the past, however, sailors traveling across the sea thought they heard strange noises.

The humming-like sounds seemed to come from the water below them.

Because of the strange sounds, the sailors told stories about sea monsters that swam near their ships.

To hear underwater sounds, a person has to be on a boat or ship that does not have a motor. Why? Noise from the motor would get in the way of being able to hear the sounds. Also, the listener should be below the deck and next to the boat's outer shell, or hull.

hull

A Whale of a Clue

For a long time, no one could explain the "sea monster" noises that sailors heard.

Then, in the 1950s, people working with the U.S. Navy made an important discovery.

They recorded loud underwater moans, grunts, squeals, and roars.

They noticed that the sounds went on for a long time—and occurred only when humpback whales were around.

Could the unusual sounds be coming from the giant animals?

scientist recording underwater sounds

hydrophone

To record underwater sounds, scientists use special microphones called hydrophones.

Singing for a Mate?

In the 1960s, scientists made more underwater recordings and found that the sounds were in fact coming from humpback whales.

The scientists also discovered that the sounds formed song-like patterns.

In addition, the singing was coming only from males.

Since the singing was heard at the time of year when whales gathered to find a **mate**, they guessed that the males might be singing to attract females.

humpback whale

blue whale

killer whale

Every kind of whale—including the blue whale, the killer whale, and the beluga whale—makes sounds. However, scientists have never recorded other whales singing songs the way humpbacks do.

Long-Distance Swimmers

Humpback whales live in all the world's oceans.

During the summer, they swim and feed in cold ocean waters near the North and South Poles.

In the fall, they spend weeks traveling to warmer waters near the equator.

These warm waters are their winter homes.

They are also the **breeding areas** where males and females find mates and males sing their songs.

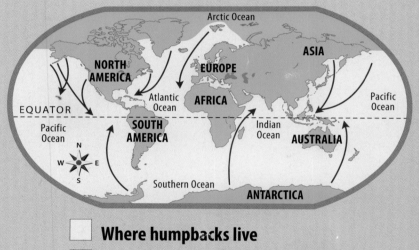

Humpback Whales in the Wild

Arctic Ocean

NORTH AMERICA
EUROPE
ASIA
AFRICA
Atlantic Ocean
Pacific Ocean
EQUATOR
Pacific Ocean
SOUTH AMERICA
Indian Ocean
AUSTRALIA
N W E S
Southern Ocean
ANTARCTICA

Where humpbacks live

→ Where humpbacks travel in the fall

Some humpback whales travel thousands of miles (kilometers) between their summer and winter homes.

Gulping Down Food

Humpbacks do not sing when they are in their summer feeding areas.

However, the huge animals do plenty of eating.

An adult humpback can eat up to one and a half tons (1,361 kg) of food a day.

Surprisingly, the 45-foot-long (14-m-long) whales eat only small fish and even smaller shrimp-like animals called krill.

humpback feeding

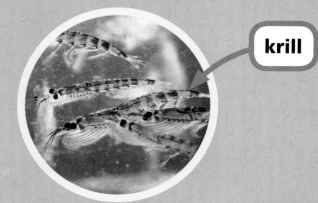

krill

Instead of teeth, humpbacks have long, thin comb-like plates called baleen in their mouths. To eat, they take big gulps of seawater. Then they squeeze out the water so that only fish and krill are left behind to swallow.

baleen

Staying in Touch

Singing is not the only way humpbacks **communicate** with one another.

Scientists have learned that the huge animals also make sounds—known as feeding calls—when they gather to catch fish.

The whales also use touch to send messages and share feelings.

For example, mother whales often use their large flippers to pet their babies, which are called calves.

mother

calf

humpback breaching

Humpback whales are known for jumping out of and back into the water—an action known as breaching. They also loudly slap the water with their flippers and tails. These splashy moves might be a way of sending messages such as "Here I am!" or "Stay out of my way!" to other whales.

Many Questions

Scientists still have many questions about humpback whale songs.

They still don't know for sure why males sing.

They also don't know exactly how the whales make their grunts, moans, roars, and many other sounds.

Other questions have to do with how the whales' feeding calls help the animals find and catch their food.

blowholes

Whales do not make sounds through their throats and mouths the way people do. Many scientists think that, instead, the big sea creatures make sounds by squeezing pockets or tubes that hold air and are located inside their bodies, near their **blowholes**.

scientists studying a humpback

A Watery World of Sound

There is one thing that scientists who study the ocean know for certain.

Sound is very important to whales and many other sea creatures.

That's because there is very little light under water, and so it is impossible to see far.

Sound, on the other hand, travels well and far through water.

So perhaps it isn't so surprising after all that songs are being sung—and heard— deep beneath the sea.

Scientists have found that humpback whale sounds can travel thousands of miles (kilometers). However, the scientists are concerned about **noise pollution** caused by ships. They think that it might harm humpbacks and other whales by making it harder for them to hear and communicate.

STAR OF MONTEREY

Sound Check

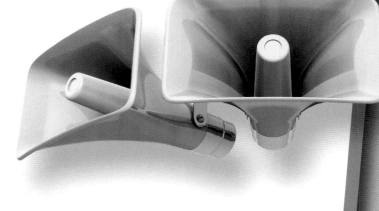

Humpback whales are hard to observe. They spend most of their time underwater, and many travel thousands of miles (kilometers) each year. Still, scientists around the world continue to study the huge sea animals and their songs. Here are some things they have learned so far:

- All the male humpbacks in the same area sing the same song.

- The songs of whales in different parts of the world are different from one another.

- During each winter breeding season, the songs of the males change, little by little.

- When the whales return to their winter homes the next year, they start singing the most recent versions of their songs from last year. Then, once again, they start changing, little by little.

Glossary

blowholes (BLOH-hohlz) openings on top of a humpback whale's head, used for breathing

breeding areas (BREED-ing AIR-ee-uhz) places in the ocean where humpback whales gather to find mates

communicate (kuh-MYOO-nuh-kayt) to pass on information, ideas, or feelings

mate (MAYT) one of a pair of animals that have young together

noise pollution (NOIZ puh-LOO-shuhn) sounds that are caused by human activities and are harmful to animals or people

Index

Read More

Jenner, Caryn. *Journey of a Humpback Whale.* New York: DK (2002).

Murray, Julie. *Humpback Whales.* Edina, MN: Abdo (2003).

Rake, Jody Sullivan. *Humpback Whales Up Close.* Mankato, MN: Capstone (2010).

Learn More Online

To learn more about humpback whales, visit
www.bearportpublishing.com/AnimalLoudmouths

About the Author

Natalie Lunis has written many science and nature books for children. She lives in the Hudson River Valley, just north of New York City.